PEOPLE BEHAVE LIKE BALLADS

BOOKS BY ROBERT P. TRISTRAM COFFIN

POEMS

CHRISTCHURCH

DEW AND BRONZE

GOLDEN FALCON

THE YOKE OF THUNDER

BALLADS OF SQUARE-TOED AMERICANS

STRANGE HOLINESS

SALTWATER FARM

MAINE BALLADS

COLLECTED POEMS

THERE WILL BE BREAD AND LOVE

PRIMER FOR AMERICA

POEMS FOR A SON WITH WINGS

PEOPLE BEHAVE LIKE BALLADS

ESSAYS

BOOK OF CROWNS AND COTTAGES

AN ATTIC ROOM

CHRISTMAS IN MAINE

BOOK OF UNCLES

MAINSTAYS OF MAINE

LECTURES

NEW POETRY OF NEW ENGLAND
(Frost and Robinson) (The Turnbull Memorial Lectures, The Johns
Hopkins University)
THE SUBSTANCE THAT IS POETRY
(The Patten Lectures, Indiana University)

BIOGRAPHIES

LAUD: STORM CENTER OF STUART ENGLAND
THE DUKES OF BUCKINGHAM
PORTRAIT OF AN AMERICAN
(The Author's Father)
CAPTAIN ABBY AND CAPTAIN JOHN
(Abby and John Pennell, Brunswick, Maine)

AUTOBIOGRAPHY

LOST PARADISE
(The Author's Life to His Twelfth Year)

NOVELS

RED SKY IN THE MORNING   JOHN DAWN
THOMAS-THOMAS-ANCIL-THOMAS

HISTORY

KENNEBEC: CRADLE OF AMERICANS
(The Rivers of America Series)

TEXTS

A BOOK OF SEVENTEENTH-CENTURY PROSE
SEVENTEENTH-CENTURY PROSE AND POETRY
(With A. M. Witherspoon)

People Behave Like Ballads

by

ROBERT P. TRISTRAM COFFIN

NEW YORK

THE MACMILLAN COMPANY

1946

PRINTED IN THE UNITED STATES OF AMERICA
BY J. J. LITTLE & IVES COMPANY, NEW YORK

ACKNOWLEDGMENTS

A few of these ballads have appeared in periodicals, and I want now to thank the editors of the following magazines for their permission to reprint them: *American Girl, Atlantic Monthly, Christian Science Monitor, Gourmet, Ladies' Home Journal, Murphy's Tavern Quarterly, National Parent-Teacher, New York Herald Tribune, New York Times, Poetry Chap-Book, Saturday Evening Post, Southwest Review,* and *Yankee.*

ROBERT P. TRISTRAM COFFIN

CONTENTS

PEOPLE BEHAVE LIKE BALLADS

STRAIGHT WORLD

Before I got up tall enough
To tell a woman from a girl,
I wore straight along my head
My mother's carefully spiralled curl.

I thought the world was pretty straight
And every needed thing near to:
North from the farmhouse stood the school,
And north of that the church spire grew.

Two miles from my bull-calves' love
And butting heads was history,
One mile more, and well-dressed men
Sang their deep bass into me.

All I had to have was there
Or somewhere on the way between,
I went due north, came home straight south,
Kept books, but not my trousers, clean.

After my yellow dog, came blue
Ocean in a sparkling bay,
And fishermen with beaded nets
And white boats met me on my way.

Next came the pinewoods deep and dark,
And if I went with care and wonder,
I met a brown deer face to face
Or sent a partridge up in thunder.

Then it was snows of Valley Forge,
Slates, loud chalk, and seven-times-seven,
Andes, and when the sun hung low,
I ran with wild boys out into heaven.

And on the seventh day I went
The one more mile there was to life,
Past white barns, white-foreheaded cows,
And sat in hymns and thought of a wife.

1

GLORY-TO-GOD EZEKIEL

Ezekiel Snodgress, six-foot-ten,
Was a mountain among men,
His beard came down a tawny thing
Like a freshet in the Spring.

His fists were sledges, but his voice
Even more made men rejoice,
It made spines stiffen like a rod—
"Glory! glory!—Glory to God!"

"Glory! glory!" Zeke would shout
When they led the big man out
To the bucksaw and the beech,
And Ezekiel made the bucksaw screech.

"Glory to God!" The sawdust flew,
Zeke was simple, but Zeke knew
God loved muscles that were taut,
God loved a bucksaw kept red-hot.

Ezekiel knew a strong man was
The apple of God, he did not pause,
He ate straight through three cords of red
Oak and went in to be fed.

A family-pot of beans, the first,
A pitcher of molasses for his thirst.
"Glory! glory!" How he ate
And ten times scoured out his plate!

A pot of peas and pork in masses,
Another pitcher of molasses.
"Glory to God!" he poured it down
And ran to the next woodpiles in town.

He saved many a puny sinner
Who watched him down his giant's dinner,
And maybe the angels now in awe
See Glory-to-God Ezekiel saw.

A GODLESS THING

They wanted a cross in place of the weather vane,
They planned to take the church's arrow down,
The times were full of freer ideas now,
They wanted to be like churches in the town.

The cross was really what the churches meant;
Their grandparents were men of narrow mind.
One farmer heard them, and his heart stood still,
Tears and anger suddenly made him blind.

Why, men for years, good men for generations
Had lifted up their eyes because they must
Know where the wind stood when they went to fish
Or plow the land.   Vanes were good things to trust.

The church spire was the highest point they had,
It stood above the highest balsam hill,
It sensed the danger in the upper air
When the Odd-Fellows' roof was in the still.

They had not thought of death and agony,
They had thought God was guardian of good hay,
Of coming home, to bring the children food,
With boatfuls of silver herring from the bay.

The plowman sent his little son to see
If wind stood in a quarter that was fair,
And many a woman looked up to the church,
With men off on the sea, as though at prayer.

The lobstering man said, "Sonny, run and look
How she stands."   The small boy, out of breath,
Came shouting shrill, "She's backing round no'theast!"
And saved his sire a twenty-fathom death.

They had no right to do this godless thing!
Why, this was turning their old folks out of graves!
A man was nearest God when, like a child,
He turned to God to know the wind and waves.

The makings of a snowstorm hung
  Before the leaden sun,
The air was full of smell of frost
  And turkey getting done.

Maybe it was the turkey smell
  That made the men give in
And take Dan to the shooting match,
  Half boy and half wide grin.

Dan's father and Dan's brothers walked
  Like lords of all creation,
But Dan walked like old Dan'l Boone
  About to found a nation.

The shooting match roared underneath
  Shubael Linscott's hill,
The moustached demigods toed the line
  And blazed away their fill.

Dan's eyes were big as two barn doors
  To hear them joke and swear,
They were full of holiday
  And walking on the air.

They shot their guns with careless grace
  Down the target's way,
They put a few shot in the sheet
  And many in the day.

Dan's people were the handsomest
  Of all the shooters there,
They almost got three mighty birds,
  But missed them by a hair.

And then Dan suddenly stood inside
  The gates of Beulah Land,
His father handed him his gun,
  "Here, Dannie, try your hand."

4

The world stopped turning on its path
  And stood as still as stone.
The men stopped moving, of all things
  Dan's muzzle moved alone.

He aimed two aeons, then one more,
  His heart clanged in his ears,
Then he fired. Someone roared,
  "There goes Linscott's steers!"

The world was full of whistling wings,
  And Dan sat down on heaven
And saw ten thousand colored stars,
  The target man yelled, "Seven!"

A silence settled deep and wide,
  Then small Dan'l heard
A voice from halfway round the world,
  "The young-one bags the bird."

At six o'clock that night a boy
  Sat shining in between
Dan'l Boone and Robin Hood
  And licked the platter clean.

GETTING THROUGH

One phrase of these plain country people
Stood up like a white church steeple
Over the common countryside,
They said it when their people died.

Old Noah Staples he got through
Just before the first snow flew,
Cheated rheumatism in his bones
By joining his cold pasture stones.

Martha Titcomb built a wall
Between her and the folks who call
To bring the gossip and lamb stew,
But the wall gave way, and she got through.

All her days as mother and wife
Eliza Snow wore out her life
Trying to reach her stony-hearted
Sons, and did, as she departed.

Simeon Lee got through with eighty
Years of lifting out the weighty
Stones from his steep hillside acres
And went to join his sturdy makers.

And maybe some souls here and there
Got through to a new place where
All time was like their childhood stories
And nothing but opened morning-glories.

FOR ONE MARRYING IN THE
HOUSE WHERE HE WAS BORN

O wise you are to happen
To wed where you were born!
The root you were and will be,
My son, is still untorn.

Your history is the apples'
Bud, blossom, and the fruit,
Son, husband, and the father,
From root to tree to root.

One year beyond Atlantic,
One past Pacific's tide,
Yet where you came to breathing
You come now to your bride.

Through wayward years and places,
The unpathed air of life,
Straight as the homing pigeon
You come home for a wife.

The lonely mortal circle
Returns and curves in right,
Two of the three man-moments
Are rounded safe this night.

The birth-bed and the bride-bed,
The one with the whispered name—
Two of the three beds waiting
All men you find the same.

O mount your bed and prosper!
Be it the third bed, too,
May thirty thousand suns rise
Before it quiets you!

It was the Summer of discontent,
The buttercups and daisies went
From Mr. Burns' doorstep to the ferns,
But they meant nothing to Mr. Burns.

Burns yearned to cut a swath in town,
He had paid ten dollars down
And had a suit of checks and tan
Shoes becoming a handsome man.

He had the build, he had the graces,
He had a pair of rosebud braces,
The conversation to inspire
The gentle sex, and tact and fire.

Mr. Burns loved the finer things,
Ties with stripes and bloodstone rings,
Nine good dollars had he squandered
On front-door lights, set kitty-cornered.

His moustache had a generous sweep,
His mind was electric, warm, and deep,
He was a figure of a male,
And had an epic thirst for ale.

There was the road to all things big,
There was his stunning red-wheeled rig,
His high-stepping sorrel, Dolly—
To bide at home was sheerest folly.

But one thing kept Burns from full vigor—
A wife, and Mrs. Burns was bigger
Than Burns was. With her, home came first,
She put it ahead of town and thirst.

So Mr. Burns with heavy hoe
Communed with turnips, row on row,
And on him burned at all his turns
The cold clear eye of Mrs. Burns.

MR. BURNS HAS A GOOD MIND
TO GO TO TOWN

The maples were all in a flame,
And Mr. Burns was much the same,
He was on fire with the Fall,
He heard the town's voice call and call.

His *savoir faire* was lost on beets,
It needed women and paved streets,
The pumpkins had nothing to say
To one who was by nature gay.

Mrs. Burns was out of sight,
The eyes of Burns brimmed with great light,
In all the house no swish of a skirt.
Burns stole upstairs to his boiled shirt.

He stole upstairs to his striped tie,
The bloodstone ring, and then the high
Box-toed shoes of ox-blood leather;
Burns brought his glories all together.

There were no moths, there were no specks
Upon the town-suit's ample checks.
Burns drew the full pants over his knees.
Good Lord!—where were the galluses?

He looked in drawers, in all the places,
He could not find his rosebud braces.
Fear drained his heart out like a cup,
Burns stood, and held his trousers up.

They were too full to go untethered,
Burns trembled, and Burns held them gathered,
But desperation lent him wings,
He inched downstairs holding the things.

And there at the stairs' foot stood like Fate
His tall icicle of a mate,
Around her waist the rosebuds wound,
And Burns' pants wilted to the ground.

9

The stars were burning through the frost,
The young new moon was going down,
A doorway opened on the night,
And Mr. Burns set off for town.

He set off quickly with his head
Ducked low down, and he went smart,
Behind him came a water pail,
It struck the snow and broke apart.

A sudden watery flower bloomed
Where Mr. Burns might well have been,
But he was halfway to the barn
In his best pair of trousers then.

Words came out behind the pail,
Woman words and close together,
But Mr. Burns was hitching up
In the smell of harness leather.

He slipped the headstall on the mare,
The sen-sen on his breath was sweet,
He made the traces fast, got in,
And headed his Dolly's nose upstreet.

Mr. Burns had had his way,
He'd got his town pants, he was free
And off for Saturday night, good ale,
And kinder female company.

Yet he could not resist the chance
To fling the last word through the door,
He drew up and flung the word
Into his house's glowing core.

He heard the taunt hit hard and deep
And cracked the whip across the mare,
His runners squealed upon the snow,
They leapt and went away from there.

But Mrs. Burns, as women will,
Was to have the last word yet,
She'd gone early to the barn
When she'd seen how the tide would set.

She'd gone there with an eagle's eye,
A handsaw, and determined tread,
She'd burned her husband's bridges so
They hung but by a slender thread.

So now when he put out his wings
To start on his victorious flight,
There came a sharp and ominous
Crack that ran across the night.

The mare went on, but not the sleigh,
Both fills broke off crisp and clean,
And Mr. Burns who held the reins
Was somewhere sadly in between.

He left the seat and joined the stars
In spite of all his lordly girth,
But his beauty was too vast,
And Mr. Burns came down to earth.

He travelled for a little time
Upon his ample chest and thighs,
He felt the snow come in and cool
His ardor and his enterprise.

The reins burned through his hands at last,
And he slowed down and came to rest,
Half the snow upon the world
Was in his trousers and his vest.

Mr. Burns lay there, the sad
Ruins of a man, and heard
The rising tumult of the last
Word and word and word and word.

MR. BURNS GOES TO TOWN

A woman's treble sharp and shrill
Shook the house from sill to sill,
The glassed door slammed like anything,
And Mr. Burns emerged in Spring.

Dandelions bloomed about his feet,
The man was dressed-up for upstreet,
Flowers across his waistcoat spread,
And Sunday's hat was on his head.

Mr. Burns lingered for no flowers,
He ran, for all his portly powers,
Faster than anyone might think,
Quick as a weasel or a mink.

Dolly was curried and harnessed there,
Nostrils already bulged with air,
The red-wheeled buggy polished sweet,
Mr. Burns vaulted to the seat.

He caught the reins as firemen do,
Cracked his whip, and he was through
The door, with Dolly showing her heels,
And out of the yard on two red wheels.

Burns was right out straight for town,
The mare's head up and his head down,
His wide moustaches stood out taut,
His whip made pistol shot on shot.

The man's head made no guilty turns,
So Burns did not see Mrs. Burns.
She had emerged like a wet hornet
All in her Sunday best and bonnet.

And as the man veered at his gate
Into freedom, into the straight,
His spouse leapt in her gown full-sail
And caught the buggy by its tail.

Off in a yellow dust they swung,
The mare, the man, the woman hung
Like a comet beyond their ken,
Her feet touched earth but now and then.

She ran little, she mostly flew,
And so the cavalcade came to
The first low houses of the town,
And Mr. Burns slowed somewhat down.

Mrs. Burns she got her purchase,
She climbed the tailboard with great lurches,
At the Congo Church she got
Her hands on the seat's back where she squat.

At the Odd-Fellows' Hall she could
Find her feet, and so she stood,
At the crowded Town-Hall Square
She got her left hand in Burns' hair.

The Saturday shoppers raised a cheer
When a tall wife blossomed sheer
From a small buggy on their sight,
Mrs. Burns got the reins in her right.

She swung the buggy round on two
Wheels, and homeward back they flew
Through Main Street, Bay Street, into the clear,
Mrs. Burns stood like Boadicea.

Back over the highway they had come,
Mrs. Burns rampant, Mr. Burns numb,
The red wheels twinkling like spinning suns,
Mr. Burns feeling like twenty tons.

The dandelions were gray-haired ghosts
In the grasses by the gateway posts,
The flowered vest was a wilted thing,
And Mr. Burns went out of Spring.

THE CROUP

The stealthy night wind tried each blind.
She could not get things off her mind:

Close to the house, by the tamaracks,
In solid rock are three-toed tracks!

Her neighbors showed her them one day,
They all pointed the house's way.

Down-cellar is the sealed-up well;
The wife went where no one can tell.

Midnight long ago had passed,
The baby was breathing fierce and fast.

Four miles to the nearest friend,
Her husband away, and none to send.

She had put the hot cloths on
Four hours, hope and strength were gone.

She sat in the hearth-fire's glow and gloom,
She could see into the baby's room.

The kettle climbed to the boiling rote,
The rattle was at the baby's throat.

She felt the fearful thing begin,
The cellar-door was opening in.

So still, so still, the silence cried,
The cellar-door came open wide.

Out of the corner of her eye
She saw the shawled one gliding by.

Cold, cold water drenched her spine,
The shawled one crossed the fire's shine.

Straight to the child the hooded went,
Over the cradle there she bent.

The hood fell over the infant's crib,
The mother's heart leaned on her rib.

Then the hooded rose and came
Face towards the fire's flame.

Now she would know what was the face!
But the shawl's hood was an empty space.

No eyes, no cheek, not any mark!
Nothing was there but dark on dark.

Death would be such, the mother knew.
She heard the cellar-door go to.

The mother sprang as wildcats spring
To the baby's crib and the dreadful thing.

The baby was smiling in his sleep,
His breath came gentle, slow, and deep.

And the window panes were growing gray,
Outside the house was holy day.

APOSTOLIC SUCCESSION

The one-roomed house was blank and bare,
And these were farmers' daughters and sons;
But this new teacher felt the air
Run with winged mysterious ones.

This was no plain New England light
The glaring empty panes let through
On scarred desks, it was unearthly white
From undersides of wings which flew.

Between the Washington in the east
And the Lincoln hung upon the west,
There was room for trumpets and feast,
And these were eaglets on a nest.

From dying hands the torch was passed,
The light went on, though runners fell,
Light was endless. He held fast
The old sharp-tongued and battered bell.

It was the school-bell which had called
His mother star-eyed from her play,
Rung by teachers who were walled
In silence now and ancestral clay.

He rang it with his mouth gone stern;
This bell within his fist was flame,
And it would call new minds to burn
When no one living knew his name.

He was of an ancient line,
Apostle of the youngest hours;
He felt the old sun in him shine,
These boys and girls were opened flowers.

THE DEMOCRATIC-REPUBLICAN CHEESE

All the farmers round Cheshire-Town
Brought the curd and pressed it down,
They sweat, they shouted in their mirth
Over the biggest cheese on earth.

Girls with arms like daisies' skin
Beat the whey and curbed it in,
Wives in Sunday-go-meeting dress
Walled in a world of toothsomeness.

Five feet across and half a ton!
Not a Federalist cow, not one,
Had any milk in it, its span
Was pure Democratic-Republican!

Only Republican Berkshire cows
Had turned tanned meadows and gold mows
Into this gift to go abroad
As common men's homage to their lord.

Big-wigs in Boston lifted high
Patrician noses towards the sky,
But Cheshire's cheese started on its way
With Parson steering the Baptist sleigh.

Down through the states the cheese slid proud,
At every village a cheering crowd
Of tinkers, carpenters, men of brawn
Sped the cheese and Parson on.

New Year's morning, 1802,
And the cheese and Parson Leland drew
Up at the house of the head of the nation
And author of the *Declaration*.

And the People's President was there,
The red of Virginia in his hair,
In buckleless shoes and Democrat black
And a smile that reached from here and back.

His hand came out to Leland's hand,
Jefferson and Liberty blared the band,
"Earth's greatest cheese," sang out the man,
"For America's greatest American!"

They put the cheese in the great East Room,
The White House burst into lovely bloom,
Ladies in skirts an acre wide,
Pottawatomies feathered in pride.

Generals, diplomats buckled and blazing,
The cheese was the center of praise and gazing,
Parson Leland, cheeked like the peach,
Unrolled his scroll and read his speech:

"This is no stone from the high Bastille,
But this cheese expresses what we feel,
This is our best, our curds and cream,
A free-will peppercorn of esteem.

"We free farmers made this thing,
We made our cheese for no proud king.
Accept it, humble though it be,
As our mite in the scale of democracy!"

Mr. Jefferson bowed to his knees,
He thanked Massachusetts for the cheese,
He took his knife and cut a slit
And gave each guest a wedge from it.

Democrats vowed it tasted fine,
Federals were sorry a divine
Was mongering cheese and whispered low
The cheese tasted only so-and-so.

But Thomas Jefferson he felt living
Tears well up, he knew he was giving,
As he cut the globe of esteem apart,
Piece after piece of a nation's heart.

18

VERMONT PRAISE

The young new preacher had an edge
Like a well-whet knife,
His eyes were full of stars as he
Spoke of eternal life.

He liked this little town in white,
The steady, sober people,
He loved this church that might be his
With mountains by its steeple.

He gave his listeners all he had,
Voice and brain and heart,
His sermon warmed him so he felt
The teardrops burn and smart.

He finished, and the hush was deep
In the little place.
A gray-haired deacon rose with calm
Vermont upon his face.

He came forward, put his hard
Hand on the preacher's arm.
"Young man," said he, "you didn't do
That text you took no harm."

The young man's face was like the sun,
The church was his, he knew,
He knew rapture when he heard it—
He was a Vermonter, too.

STEPHEN BENÉT

We shall recall him always where white
American thunderheads stand up from night,
Always when wind brings the hunting horn,
And American asters stand by the corn.

New Hampshire will mind us, his Dan'l drove
The Devil from her sweet maple grove,
Maple trees never will burst into flame
But they will light up his American name.

His name is now the echo in hills,
Cabin smoke rising, sad whippoorwills,
Fiddles and quick feet shaking a floor,
And the ghostly god in the sycamore.

For he was American as they come,
As *Yankee Doodle* or Seneca drum,
As bayberry candles, yarrow and sorrel,
And the May-night blizzards of mountain laurel.

He could sing light as the deer in the dew,
Deep as the thunder that Gettysburg knew,
High as the clouds where bald eagles hang,
Whatever he wrote, always he sang.

Safe with the eagle, the seal of our state,
Safe in the lilacs where thrushes mate,
He with Walt Whitman goes singing along,
Safe in the heart of American song.

GOD COMING HOME

Each time her husband broke his vow
She belled him home like a truant cow,
Ahead of his befuddled feet
A boy with a cowbell woke the street.

The people sprang out of their beds,
At all the windows there were heads,
Good men and women gazed with scorn
At the poor slave of John Barleycorn.

The man with whiskey at his heart
Walked the street with legs apart,
Swayed here and yon from door to door,
And the belling boy marched straight before.

This was New England, this was just,
Good citizens paraded lust
To make bad children all turn over
The leaf, and glorify Jehovah.

The man had lightning in each eye,
His head was like a ram's held high,
He felt the toes upon him curled
Around the great curve of the world.

And one boy of a five-year size
Stared from his window all wide eyes
And saw no sin and saw no night
But only a streetful of vast light.

It was the town's foremost disgrace,
It was light on a small boy's face
Who saw his sire, gray as a mouse,
Come home a god to his small house.

THE SPRING

The sick man wanted just one thing:
Water. Water from one spring.

One certain spring high in the hills,
Neighbor to the whippoorwills.

It bulged from out the ferny ground
Like a diamond cut out round.

Last time he saw it, his feet were bare
And pine-spills in his boyish hair.

Half a hundred years ago,
And it still came up cool as snow.

So close to sky, the spring ran blue—
One drink from that high pool would do.

All its bubbles were alive
As honey-bees are in a hive.

One swallow of it would erase
Age and the fever on his face.

He told his wife with deep eyes burning,
He told his secret and his yearning.

The woman climbed the hill, but found
No diamond bulging from the ground.

The way was rough and laced with briars,
The sun danced on the leaves like fires.

She scratched her hands, she tore her dress,
She came home full of weariness.

She filled the pitcher at the well,
Her man was sick, he could not tell.

The water was cool enough, it gleamed,
The pool was something he had dreamed.

The man drank once, and that was all.
He turned for good towards the wall.

NEW BOY IN THE OLD HOUSE

Here in the white old house he sits
A young new blond boy, yet he fits
Into four handsome men who wore
This head of hair of his before.

He is all there is beneath the skies
Of his great-grandfather's sea-bright eyes,
His grandfather's chin and eager nose,
Through five good men this brave chin goes.

Four boys before him learned to climb
These steep, hard stairs in their good time
And came to high rooms, women's lips,
Honor, vast plans, the square-rigged ships.

Two builders of ships each side his bed,
A century of sun upon his head,
A master-builder on the stair;
He breathes in fine men with the air.

Every chair he sits on makes him
More of his fathers, each step takes him
Back to the white past as he goes
Into years coming with chiselled nose.

How can a boy not grow up sound
With such men to become around?
Room by wide room, wake or sleep,
He fills the white bright house they keep.

Two in the bone-orchard should be
For each one in the orchard tree—
That is the proper ratio;
New England's small towns prove it so.

A man will toe the hard mark right
When he is in his grandmother's sight,
Though his grandmother is a granite
Shaft where all who pass may scan it.

Small boys will mind their P's and Q's
And not wade puddles in good shoes
When he who made and loved them lies
Under the grassy hill all eyes.

Ten men quiet for one in love;
When straight old good men lie above
A white town they kept neat as a pin,
It will be hard for a man to sin.

New England dead are not the dead,
They are judges of heart and head;
And he who knows them has a start
On a character and a heart.

It's no wonder New England raises
Good men common as white daisies;
The best ones here are granite stones,
And granite's a model for young bones.

THE IDYLL OF MARS McMANUS

Jim Decovin, skipping school,
Saw it at McManus' pool
When he was tickling rainbow trout,
And Jim's eyes almost both popped out.

Then Raphael Doughty's little Tim,
Who'd had the birthday pants on him
Warmed by Mars McManus' paw
For swimming in his water, saw.

Next, Dan Trefethen saw the sight,
But Dan was less than halfway bright.
But when John Morgan saw it, too,
Folks sat up, and tongues all flew.

That such a thing could be in Maine!
Why, they might be right smack in Spain!
And Bethel's good name would be gone
If towns nigh heard such goings-on.

The farmers at the cracker-box
Allowed that unless Sheriff Cox
Did something to avert the shame,
Someone was going to lose her name.

For Mars McManus' place was no
Fit place for a girl to grow,
There were too many tykes with red
Hair the shade of Mars' big beard.

How, by golly, could they be
Sure it was a she, not he?
What with nothing to judge it by
Save one single—er—er—thigh?

Why, they were all of them she-creatures,
And they all had the needful features,
Swore Sam Snow and blushed beet-red,
It was in the books he'd read.

But Swede Jensen said, "No, Sir!"
Those single ladies of Sam's were
Saltwater ones, the freshwater kind
Had pairs as good as you would find.

He knew they had forked limbs because
There a lovely forked one was
On his family tree curled tight—
Far back enough to be all right.

"Maybe that explains your scales,"
Hen Pennell laughed, but Waitstill Fales
Swore no scales were ever seen
On Jensen's kind, the true undine.

"But Johnny Morgan saw scales there,
When she was combing her green hair
On the sand-bar. He said they
Were like thick bluets late in May."

"It ain't no undine, it's a strayed
Pretty, innocent mermaid
Who came from Back Bay last neap tide
And couldn't get back when she tried."

But all agreed they must keep quiet
For fear red-bearded Mars might spy it,
And made the boys agree to wear
Trunks when they went swimming there.

But Mars McManus must have heard
The secret from some tattle-bird;
The boys saw naked Mars wade under
His pool with beard out like the thunder.

And thunder came without a rain,
One puff of wind lodged Sam Snow's grain,
Jensen's Guernsey swallowed her cud,
His woman cracked an egg pure blood.

Jens got his overalls on back to
And found it out when set to do
Something needful. Lightning hit
John Darling's vane and melted it.

Sarah Woodside digging new
Potatoes found one made with two
Legs and other marks of a man,
And shrieked, upset her pail, and ran.

And after the dark and bone-dry shower,
The east turned morning-glory flower,
The biggest rainbow ever noted
With one leg on Mars' water floated.

All the thrushes started to sing
As though 'twere evening and still Spring,
The sky was filled with golden bees,
And some folks heard bells in the trees.

When Mars McManus, wide of beam,
Went down into his little stream,
The boys said that the pool rose four
Feet and frothed white, shore to shore.

Anyway, Mars' Jerseys lowed
Knee-deep where the water flowed
Over the lower meadow's clover
As though a cloudburst were just over.

The boys got their knee-breeches wet,
They tried hard, but they could not get
A good look at what went on after,
It snowed white foam, and there was laughter.

But in the sunset Mars came home,
His wide red beard was full of foam,
His naked muscles shone like gold,
He sang, and wheels of thunder rolled.

After that day, no boy fished
Mars' brook, though giant rainbows swished
Their spotted tails there, for the great
McManus swam there early and late.

But toddling boys grow up in time,
And other boys in their bright prime,
When death old Mars McManus took,
Dropped in the pool a squirming hook.

They had great bites, but when they yanked
Fit to split the cloth pa spanked,
The hook came up without a thing,
Clean as a mud-wasp's bluish sting.

They fished an hour, still no luck,
They all at once stared thunderstruck,
The pool broke into ten wide grins
Of boys with wide ears that were fins!

The boys in breeches did not wait
For lines or poles or can of bait,
They did not wait to see what flopped
Where the mer-boys' back-struts stopped.

And that is why the rainbow trout
Swim Mars Brook year in, year out,
And slap the pool with carefree tails
Until they grow as big as whales.

People give the pool wide berth,
They say at twilight time shrill mirth
Shakes the willows with gay noise
From redhead Yankee water-boys.

FIRE DRAWS FIRE

I told you once, I tell you again:
Don't build your house where fire's been.

She kept her house all scrubbed and neat,
The most particular eater could eat
Off her floors. She did not marry,
For men and children always carry
Dirt into the house when they return.
What could a fire find to burn
In a place picked up so well?
But burn it did, the ridgepole fell
On her in the midst of sleep.

I guess her going so will keep
Folks from building any more
On that cellar. They built before.
They never told her, but that nice
House of hers had been built twice.
Once for her mother, once for her.
They saved the baby when they were
Trying to save the baby's mother.
She burned to death all right, that other.
And now the house has got the one
It missed before, and that is done.

I told you once, I tell you again:
Don't build your fire where fire's been.

THE RED DRUMMER

The night the silk bursts from the maize
And northern lights send up their blaze,
The drumming comes, and girls and boys
Run to the woodland and the noise;
Girls with breasts like apples hark
To the deep drum beating in the dark,
Forgetting drums are dangerous to hear
When the corn is in the ear.

At the highwater mark of Summer
People hear the ghostly drummer.
It's the red-haired lad in buff-and-blue
Who drummed the charge against the crew
Of George the Third's tall men in red,
He drums still, though two centuries dead,
So Castine people say, and nod;
But the drum beats like the heart of God.

No house can hold the girls, no mothers,
Laws or lamplight, books or brothers;
Girls dance with strange boys in the gloom,
And tall corn stands erect in plume.
The girls come homeward, red and wise,
And walk the year with averted eyes;
They talk no more of drums or noise,
But carry in Spring their red new boys.

Some wise ones at white dawn have seen
Who it is that drums between
The cornrows. He is no boy's kind,
His eyes are turquoises and blind,
He wears feathered lightning on his head,
The corn ears bow before his tread.
He is a god, the earth shakes under
His Indian drum that makes the thunder.

THREE CITIZENS OF BRUNSWICK

In the long annals of the ages
One man can carry few of the pages
In his mind. Our town is old,
More than three hundred years have rolled
Over Brunswick since the first
White man knelt to slake his thirst
In irised springs that seem to rise
From crystal-hearted Paradise,
A thousand gales with level snow,
Three hundred sudden Junes to blow
Wild roses open on the Plains,
More than ten thousand rains to trail
Beads of raindrops and the hail.

Three hundred years is a long time
To be pressed into a rhyme,
So let us out of many days
Choose us three alone in praise
Of citizens who went before.
Three out of many citizens
Who have made us proud of men's
Daring to stand up and be
Between Androscoggin and the sea.
Three days from three centuries,
And our citizens are these:

One is a boy of eight years old
  With fear in his eyes like high thunder,
One is a ship that girdled the globe,
  And one an old man going under.
One is a lad alive as a lynx,
  And one is a ship for a story,
And one an old teacher who stayed home and taught
  And walked a Maine beach into glory.
A teacher, a ship, a boy close to earth
  Who grew up a tower of a man—
These are the citizens whom I shall take
  From Brunswick's three-century span.

Tip-top high tide at Maquoit,
   High noon of the day,
The butter of the buttercups
   Spilled into the bay.

Seventeen-hundred, twenty-two,
   A land alive with Summer,
On every daisy of the field
   Drummed a tiny drummer.

The sweetness of the year poured out
   Deep honey in the sun,
In woods behind the English hay
   Lean death came on the run.

"Matthew, Son, the kine are home!
   What can ail the kine?
Mistress Woodside's baking bread
   Right at noonday shine!

"Neighbor Woodside's chimney smokes
   Like a house afire.
Look!—Mistress Woodside's running out
   In her span-new tire!"

James Thornton stood upon the land
   He'd turned from trees to sod,
His Scotch-Irish mouth went wide,
   "God!" he said, "Good God!"

The Woodside house smoked everywhere,
   Gable, ridgepole, pane,
Three naked men sprang up and seized
   The woman in the grain.

Matthew Thornton saw one man
   Lift his arm and chop,
His eight-year eyes saw woman's hair
   Come off by the top.

Neighbor Woodside ran for life,
   Guns puffed, he gave a yell,
Men like dark bluebottle flies
   Swarmed where Woodside fell.

Men with bodies like bright snakes,
   Striped with gold and red,
Crested with the eagle's wings
   On their tufted head.

Men as quick as quicksilver
   And sinews like the granite,
Men like insects in dim dreams,
   Men from another planet.

Son Matthew's eyes were like the blue
   Of sky where thunder comes,
He put his hand in father's hand,
   He heard the bees' small drums.

James Thornton came back to the world
   From hell and far away,
"Quick, lad, the cove, and look alive!
   Our only chance's the bay."

James called his wife, they turned their backs
   On all they had to save,
Wheat and house and home, they turned
   From a yawning grave.

The birch canoe was in the vetch,
   A kingfisher screamed and flew,
One sweep of James Thornton's arms,
   And they rocked on the blue.

They hugged the shore and held their breath,
   Heads down below the thatch,
They pulled themselves along with hands
   Red with many a scratch.

Not once did man, wife, son look back,
    But their house came in smoke
After them, it brought the tears
    And made them gasp and choke.

They heard the cows low deep, forlorn,
    Daisy, Moll, and Beth,
Bidding them farewell from throats
    Touched by the edge of death.

The blue edge of the afternoon
    Covered them with gloom,
Past Bunganuc, past oak and pine,
    They crept away from doom.

Goodbye to blue Maquoit, goodbye
    To days like crystal stones,
Farewell to nights of northern lights,
    Farewell, the hearth's dear stones!

When evening lay out long and deep
    And marsh-hens walked their pickets,
They reached the tip of Flying Point
    And hid them in spruce thickets.

The bright brain of the little boy
    Crowded drear with dreams,
Men with feathers for their hair
    And hatchets sharp as screams.

And the father had to take
    The boy's head on his arm,
Cover his face away from the stars
    And smooth away the harm.

Now and then a lonely howl
    Trembled below the stars
Where far to northward evil glares
    Marked the night like scars.

Next day with famine at their side
　　They paddled the bold water,
Past Chebeague, and past the smoke
　　Of Falmouth and dark slaughter.

Down the long coast and the ruins
　　Of all Maine's hopes and people,
Not a door with faces in it,
　　Not a church's steeple.

The pious, white and godly homes
　　Gone into the blue,
On every thrifty Scottish hearth
　　The barbed wild thistle grew.

So they left Maine's coast forever
　　And came at last inside
The arm of Portsmouth and went up
　　Weary from the tide.

That little son James Thornton saved
　　From death in blue Maquoit
Grew and took his place among
　　Our nation's strong and great.

A famous doctor, he stood up
　　And helped to found a nation,
When they needed men to dare,
　　He signed the *Declaration*.

A small and quiet place in Maine
　　May breed a thunderful son,
Maine has bred a thousand such,
　　And Matthew is but one.

A century and a half slide like a stream,
A watch within the night, like a quick dream.

The old Maquoit Road smoked from town to sea
With carriages, buckboard and carryall,
Old ladies under fringe and canopy,
Buggies and red wagons loaded low
To their gunwales with pent dynamite
Of boys with deep blue morning in their eyes.

The year was at its heaviest with fruit,
The road was edged with flames of maple trees.
Down Pennell's Wharf Road moved the laughing town
In striped trousers, hoops, and holiday,
Past the eight mansions of the Pennell Brothers,
Past lawns and houses that the Greeks might dream.
Brunswick was on foot, on hoof, on wheels,
The sun was climbing high towards the noon,
The tide was run its highest of the year.

October twenty-seventh, seventy-four,
The largest ship of Brunswick high on shore.

Under the arches of the frost-struck elms,
Higher than the eaves upon the house
Beside it there, the great new ship stood still
Between the billows of the Queen Anne's lace—
A thousand and four-hundred, thirty-three
Good tons of good white Maine, ten thousand oaks
Which once held sky up on their mighty heads,
Two hundred feet of curves and loveliness,
Built to the music of the Yankee mind,
Built in the time of daisies, full of Summer,
Shaped to the waves and Winter and vast storms,
Fitted to the curving of the world,
A citizen of Leghorn and Cadiz,
Callao and the Horn and Sunda Straits.
The *Benjamin Sewall*, youngest Pennell ship,
And greatest of them all, keen for the sea!

Above the words of women and men,
Brunswick's greatest citizen,

Waiting the word to slip her down
And go forever from the town.

All was ready for holiday
Once the ship was on the bay,
The tables spread below the trees,
Blackberry jam swarmed round with bees,
Cold turkey meat, cold ham and beef,
Gilt pumpkin pies beyond belief,
Chicken breast and raspberry shrub,
And cream and butter by the tub;
Cinnamon cookies and sugared buns,
And all the plates like little suns.
Boys all emptiness and yearning,
Sunlight on the glassware burning.
Parasols bobbing with cobweb lace,
Old men with youth upon their face,
Fringed blue gentians opened wide,
A million minnows at rim of tide,
Children thick as frostflowers there,
The ship on the ways, wind blowing fair!

The *Benjamin Sewall* starting out on life,
The man who named it at the end of his,
A man with eighty frosts upon his hair
On the deck. True twelve upon the clock,
Time and the tide at full. The President
Of Bowdoin College, Joshua Chamberlain,
Who turned the Rebel tide at Gettysburg,
Who took the sword surrendered by great Lee,
With wind in his long hair, stood on the sky,
Stood on the high top-gallant forecastle.
He called for silence, and the thousand there
Fell quiet, and they heard the seagulls call
Beyond the headland, over Middle Bay.
Captain John Pennell, Abby, and their son
Stood on the curving climax of their life,
Stood by the President. But down below
Their other son stood blinded by his tears
Because he was afraid that they would go

And leave him sole alone.   Another child,
A Pennell daughter, in an apple tree,
Wept behind the bandage on her face,
To think her ailing eyes had shut her off
From seeing something that would break her heart.
The preacher and the teacher, John S. Sewall,
Of Bowdoin, lifted up his voice and prayed:

> God of the sun and moon and stars!
> Be with this ship, these men,
> Hold them in Thine hollow hand
> And bring them home again.
>
> God of our grandsires and our sons!
> Go with this ship to sea,
> Do not suffer sails to take
> Thy children from Thy knee.

Across the silence the high prayer rang,
And then a hundred mauls and hammers sang,
Rose in a mighty anthem of quick blows,
Then stopped. A single last stroke. "There she goes!"
No one believed it for a moment's space,
And then the great thing moved in lonely grace,
Came alive and glided down the hill,
Hit the sea and turned it to a mist
Of crystal and slow hills of amethyst
Curling up behind it either way,
And stood up true and proud on the golden day.
The son on land ran after it until
His breath gave out, he stood and saw it glide
Half the world away upon the tide.
His cousin Carroll, Master James's son,
Tried to throw his hat up at the fun,
But the elastic underneath his chin
Anchored his sailor to him like all sin,
It slipped down like a blindfold on his eyes
And smothered up his mouth and lusty cries.
Three cheers went up and made the elm boughs shake,
The beauty of it made a man's heart ache,

The ship stood on the ocean, white and tall,
The highest and the handsomest ship of all!

No one heard the whisper passed,
"The loveliest, and it is last.
Last of the ships of Pennellville,
Last of the ships to climb the hill,
The blue Atlantic hill, and go
Around the globe in sun and snow,
Last of the line of a century,
The loveliest, last ship there will be."

No one heard Time speak and say
Something of another day
When this captain proud of tread
Would lie in Rio Harbor dead.

Nobody heard through the thick world
The breakers on Formosa curled
Where this ship would break her heart,
Where her ribs would fall apart.

All that people heard was joy,
Above the crying of a boy,
And they cheered again, again,
This white-oak citizen of Maine.

Ten years pass, June of eighteen-eighty-four,
And I have come to this one moment more
In the story of our town's long past,
And this the benediction and the last.

ALPHEUS SPRING PACKARD

The year was done. His Baccalaureate
Was now in history with his other ones,
He had seen the Seniors rise and go
And join his sixty-five tall sets of sons.

Sixty-five years made a good long day,
It was June, the teacher now could rest,
Alpheus Packard walked along the shore
And watched the bright sun sloping down the west.

Books had been his life, his mother read
Pope's *Odyssey* while pacing, carding wool,
She had taught him love of books, his mind
Was full of precepts, and his heart was full.

He had been the town's first citizen
Many years, and had his hand in laws,
He had loved the light beyond all else,
The college year was done, and he could pause.

He had preached the funeral farewell
To many fine sea captains home from sea,
To Captain John D. Pennell, who had died
Where Rio's mountains preach eternity.

He had walked the chapel pathway home
To his house on College Street so long
The walking and the chapel had become
A part of him, and something like a song.

Now he paced the Squirrel Island shore,
He saw the spruces that were made like lace,
Death came and met him suddenly like a friend,
He lay with the blue sea-light on his face.

General Chamberlain bade the man farewell
In the church where Packard's light had shone,
"One sphere of life fulfilled, God took him higher,
Walking by the seashore, he walked on."

And these are three good citizens our town
Has bred our land: A boy who won renown,
A mighty ship which rode through storms and calms,
A man who strayed from one of David's psalms.

41

In all the blueberry-bogs and spruce
Of Washington County was no prouder
Selectman of a fog-bound town
Than Jeremiah Calvin Crowder.

His little place was mossy rocks,
Ten houses where a stream spilled down,
But Jerry was the Pericles,
The First Selectman of his town.

Columbia Falls was starry space,
He felt a nation on his shoulders
And not the taxes or sardines
In this town all boats and boulders.

Yet this tall ruler had one flaw,
And Fate found out the spot and hit.
Jerry loved whiskey, and he walked
Taller and prouder thanks to it.

But one black night he went abroad
To add to his inches with the stuff,
And in the freedom from state cares,
In a foreign place, took more than enough.

He could not recall what laws he broke,
He racked his brains to no avail.
But there he was, a prince of men,
Cooped, cribbed, confined in Eastport's jail!

He shook the house with his vast hands,
He filled the deep night with loud bawls,
"You cannot do this thing to me,
I'm the Head Man in Columbia Falls!"

No one came. His cries thinned out,
His inches dwindled to the dawn.
And when they sent him home next day,
A man named Pericles was gone.

GIRLS BY THE ROAD

Genevieve, Alice, Lucy, and Kate,
They crowd by the road the people go,
Ann and Emma, Elvira and Nell,
Eight longing girls in a breathless row.

The river runs blue in meadows behind,
But they face the roadway going to town,
Peepers ring clear as small silver bells,
But girls think little of settling down.

Girls love the twinkle of carriages' wheels
And horses with wide noses afire,
The tall young men with arrogant minds
As alone as roses in the briar.

Their mother knew the road was the thing,
She herself came from over the hills,
And so as her daughters came to their time
She let the slim daughters have their wills.

The mountains are haunting, and a thrush
Sings like a seraph snared in a tree,
Home is for old-ones, babies, and peace,
But a road is where girls love to be.

So eight girls unwilling ever to grow
Gray-haired or thickened in their bones
Line the road the people take,
The sunlight picks out their eight stones.

Nell, Elvira, Emma, Ann
Announce their names and stand and shine,
Kate, Lucy, Alice, Genevieve,
Eight longing girls in one white line.

THE WATERMELON PRESERVES

The mountain boy with breathing holes
In the two cushions at his seat
And two teeth missing at the front
Had one good tooth—that was his *sweet*.

His eyes were quick as cherrybirds,
His mouth as wide as Tennessee,
He'd get outside a watermelon
That weighed about the same as he.

His ma kept a three-gallon jar
Of her best watermelon preserves
On her pantry shelf in case
She'd need to call out the reserves.

Jim scented out ma's secret there,
He took off the cheesecloth top,
He sampled what he found, and found
No earthly way that he could stop.

But there would be another day,
And so when he was part way down,
Jim sighed to think he was so small
And put back on the jar's white gown.

Next day Jim sampled once again,
The next and next and next and next,
He put the cloth top back each time
So his ma would not be vexed.

Then suddenly one bitter day
Jim found that all was gone but juice,
He dredged with woebegone big eyes,
Then he slipped back the cheesecloth noose.

Sunday, ma had company,
"You-all must try my melon rind."
All up the mountain side was dust
A small and pale boy left behind.

For two years when ma would declare
She did not see how rats could eat
Three gallons of watermelon jam,
Jim goosefleshed up and down his seat.

But one day Jim confessed to ma
He was the rat that ate the jam,
And ma said, "Well, I vum! I ought
To give your breeches one good lam!"

But ma had not the heart to spank
When Jimmie grinned and spoke up coy,
"You lost your watermelon jam,
But, ma, you had that much more boy!"

THE MORMON HOUSE

Here stands the house a Mormon planned
A bedroom lies on either hand.

There are bees and honey on my mouth,
Love me, O North! Love me, O South!

I am the mountain goat in the dew,
My love is comely, and is two!

I am the Spring! Undo to the ram
Thy twin gates, O Jerusalem!

The house the Mormon built this way
Houses spinsters this latter day.

Two ancient virgins lie alone
In rooms love flowered once in stone.

No ram, no Spring comes ever here,
Lonely year follows lonely year.

Behold, I am comely, daughters of Zion,
I am the gold-eyed running lion.

Swing your doors and gateways wide,
Each room will blossom with a bride.

A virgin is a brief small thing,
Open, O gates, to your tall king!

And all that enters to that house
Is a gray and truant mouse.

He makes no louder sound than tears,
The house is crumbling under the years.

BOY'S LAMP

The boy was lying still, but he was hot,
Wrath was in bed with him.   The boy had got
The lamp blown out on him, with Indians creeping
On the log-cabins and the people sleeping.

He had to know what happened. He could not sleep,
He went in his white night-tails down the steep
Stairway.   No one stirred in all the house
Except a little truant, hungry mouse.

The stars were large as lanterns in the elms,
He held his tails up, not to wet the hems
With the dew, his thighs felt strange with night
Around them and no breeches holding tight.

He got a bottle by the woodshed wall,
The field beyond was not his field at all,
It was ten times wider with the dark,
And it was afire, spark on spark on spark.

He caught the wandering fires where they rested
And lit the grasses up where they were crested,
He put them in his bottle one by one,
He held a glowing lamp when he was done.

The bearer of the light crept back to bed,
He put his lamp close to the page and read.
The lightning-bugs inside could not agree
On sparking all at once, but he could see.

By intermittent flashes Redskins ran
Smoking with the scalps of many a man,
The boy read on with mouth and blue eyes wide
While night held up her living lamp beside.

HORN HENS

Cap'n Obadiah Black,
When Spring was climbing up the globe,
Sailed s'uth'ard with his Plymouth Rocks,
His wife, and small sons, John and Job.

They were all on tiptoe then
For Summer clothes, the heat, green-corn,
And Obadiah plunged them all
Into white Winter off the Horn.

John and Job were chock, chock full
Of Old Nick, sulphur-and-molasses,
They got a shock that made their tails
Droop like the October grasses.

Mrs. Obad shrank up, too,
Took jibs in, battened down, and bolted;
But the poor dumbfounded hens
Could not reverse—they up and moulted!

In blank amaze the hens looked round
At their back parts in the chill air,
The tears welled in their rounded eyes,
For there was nothing, nothing there!

They stood naked in the wild
White and wintry Cape Horn weathers,
They could not scratch, they could not sing,
Could not be mothers, lacking feathers.

The cap'n's wife got out her shears
And cut the cap'n's pants in slivers,
She made small canvas jackets, too,
To stop the biddies' desperate shivers.

The great Horn Mountains stood and roared
Fit to burst their iron stitches,
They saw a crew of hens go by
In canvas coats and blue serge britches!

WATER-DIVINER

They did not believe, they smiled to see him,
A small and light, white-headed man
Going about with his forked willow
And telling men where the water ran!

A southwest wind, if it caught him proper,
Could take him up like a milkweed wing,
Yet his willow wishbone bowed and twisted
In his clenched fists, a living thing.

He held it tight till his knuckles whitened,
Yet the willow moved against men's laws,
They shook their heads, but got their shovels,
And there the living water was!

A small old man with a boy's strange plaything
Out of a time when times were young
And believed in fairies, arks, Jehovahs,
Big families, and an old man's tongue.

He did not know about his power,
He only knew that it was there,
As the small boy knows the girl will worship
If he stands enough upon his hair.

The man was humble, it wasn't his doing,
He was an agent, no master at all,
There are certain trees, not all trees growing,
Down which the lightnings choose to fall.

Why two limbs to his branch of willow?—
He noticed when man works or woos,
Walks or looks or climbs or listens,
Most of his instruments come by twos.

His work was silent, it made him sober,
He gripped his fork with forking thighs,

He went slow, and he went patient,
All his life was in his eyes.

Look!—The process was beginning!
The green barb sharpened by his knife
Went over slow and fierce and pointed
Like a finger at running life.

BATTLE OF RAMS

It was a sorry day for Wright
When Son Tom shot up his height.

Tom Wright was headstrong as a ram
In the Spring, and so was Sam.

Son and father had one thought:
To go where the other decided not.

They were crossed sticks all the day
On the clamflats, in the hay.

Sam had tried to break Tom's will,
But only made it tougher still.

They were knotty red, red oak,
They would stand till something broke.

Now the fateful day will rise
When son reaches father's size.

And so it rose on Sam and Tom,
A blue May day, bright as a bomb.

The two were ready to put out
To lobster-pots set roundabout.

They launched the dory, piled in stores,
Took their seats, and rigged the oars.

Now, the dory, between friends,
Is a boat with two bow-ends.

And this day Tom did not take seat
With his back towards father's feet.

The days when he must pull stern oar
Were gone with knee-pants forevermore.

He put his feet against his sire's,
And glared at him, his eyes were fires.

Sire'd decided to pull west,
But son had a mind the east was best.

They said no word, they sat and faced
Each other, feet to big feet braced.

They bent their broad backs and gave way,
The dory quivered, sway on sway.

But it did not go ahead,
It stayed and rolled and rocked instead.

The father put on extra steam
And strained his pants at every seam.

The son called on his extra gristle
And made his oarlocks' leather whistle.

They were a handsome, equal pair,
And they rowed, and went nowhere.

The sun rose higher, tide turned flood,
The two rowed flushed with gimp and blood.

The lobsters ate a dinner free,
Imprisoned under the cold sea.

The men rowed on, there was no shift.
The boat made only a natural drift.

But its swaying, anguished motion
Took the boat out on the ocean.

And all Hen Harbor had clear view
Of what had happened to these two.

Men dropped their hammers from their paws,
Dropped their cuds from open jaws.

Small boys with bright saucer eyes
Danced and let out treble cries.

They cheered the Wrights, they yelled to brothers,
They legged it home and told their mothers.

Every woman dropped her pies,
The window panes were full of eyes.

The Wrights rowed on without a shame
Giving Hen Harbor a bad name.

A son and father, set as mules,
Rowing opposite like two fools!

A two-stemmed dory like a dunce
Trying to go two ways at once!

The sun slid down, and still they tugged,
Their arms-joints creaked, their blue eyes bugged.

No knowing when they would have stopped
If the ebb tide hadn't dropped.

In the light of the earliest star
The dory's bottom hit the bar.

They felt the mud, they let up rowing,
They sat there with their nostrils blowing.

Young Thomas moved the first, he stood,
Waded ashore and packed for good.

The criss-cross partnership was done,
It was lone father and lone son.

But people in Hen Harbor mind
That race of two rams of a kind.

They tell how rowers kicked up foam
All one day and stayed at home!

The crew of Cap'n Peter Murphy
Were Tartars mixed with rattlesnakes,
They soured Cap'n Peter's milk
With their brawls and bellyaches.

One day, Jens Jensen fought a fight
With the Red Scourge, Tim O'Shea,
Tim pulled his knife upon the Swede
And laid his "innerds" bare to day.

Cap'n Peter yelled, "Run quick
And fetch a marlinspike to me!"
He hit the opened man a blow
That laid him stiff as charity.

The patient thus anesthetized,
Peter got his curved sail-needle,
Shoved Jens' entrails in, and sewed
Him up again tight as a fiddle.

In two weeks' time, the Swede was up
In the yards as good as new
And putting his knuckle marks upon
The rattlesnake-and-Tartar crew.

And Cap'n Peter Murphy's milk
Of human kindness was still tart
When he saw how small regard
His men had for his big warm heart.

GRANDMA WAS THE FUTURE

Grandmother Goodnow lived when pants
Were checked with Victorian elegance,
When wives were built like hourglasses,
When lads wore curls like little lasses.

But Grandmother Goodnow did not look
Back to the good old times, she took
An onion out of her whistling gown
At Browning meetings and munched it down.

She did not know the vitamins,
But she said sun was good for skins
And took off corsets, stripped to the waist
On fine days, and was not disgraced.

She walked stately as a queen
In iridescent bombazine
But had her ten toes all in use,
Curved to the world in tennis-shoes.

When other wives used smelling-salts,
She turned somersaults, vaulted vaults,
Swung dumbbells and the Indian clubs,
And rolled her fat off over tubs.

She did not sing the lovesick tunes,
She had a yearning for balloons,
Her people had to lock the bars
To keep her from scraping off the stars.

She vowed a buggy was a sad
Vehicle, and she'd be glad
When men turned horses out to grass
And rode in buggies pushed by gas.

Grandchildren tried to be her kind,
But they were always miles behind,
They sprouted corns, they fell half-dead—
Grandma kept fifty years ahead.

THE CLEAN CAPTAINS

No matter where they sailed their ships,
The Yankee captains lean of hips
Carried the religion and the grace
Of their clean and decent place.

Guano, lumber, sugar, coal—
It mattered not, they carried soul
As well as substance, carried mind
To the ports of humankind.

They took their wives and setting hens
And thought they carried beds and pens,
But carried the warm breasts of creation
And handsome life that meant a nation.

They carried babies bright as thunder
Sleeping stoutly still in under
The bellied sails and planning an earth
Far greater than their money's worth.

They thought their wives were mending pants,
But mending turned into romance,
Their women rocked in rocking-chairs
And turned ideas out by the pairs.

They took independence in their eyes,
Ambition to rise, and pumpkin pies,
They carried order on their path,
Thrift, and the Saturday evening bath.

Sailors filled half-hogsheads full
For the New England ritual
Of Saturday night and soap and rub,
And small boys stood up in the tub.

Grinning sailors poured the sea
On small heirs of infinity,
Naked New England boys stood white
Against immense Pacific night.

This was a service all as fine
As any sweet with corn and wine
That used to mingle youth and bliss
Under the old Acropolis.

The Yankees worked their bodies lean,
They found and left the ocean clean,
They left us something hard as nails
And somewhat whiter than their sails.

THE BRIGHT HALF-BRIGHT

Jonas Bye, the half-bright boy,
Was Aurora's pride and joy,
He said things at ten which gray
Men would give ten years to say.

When Presbyterians by pairs
Marched into church with Sunday airs,
Jonas stood outside and crew,
"The animals went in two by two!"

The boy was the sparkle and the yeast,
He made the dullest day a feast,
Seeing him run for running's sake
Cured many a chronic stomach-ache.

Then one day all the sparks died down,
A big new family moved to town,
And they had a half-bright boy whose mind
Was light as the heels he kicked behind.

Jonas's nose was out of joint,
He sat out on Fish-House Point
Watching the lake's waves as they went,
He sulked like Achilles in his tent.

One day, the new clan raised great sound
Of woe. Their boy could not be found.
Folks searched the woods, the hills, Payne's Creek,
They scoured the county for a week.

Word came at last from the other side
Of Lake Cayuga, blue and wide,
Had someone lost a half-bright lad?
They had one there, lonesome and sad.

It all came out then clear as snow,
Jonas enticed the boy on a row
Over the lake and left him alone
To build up an empire of his own.

58

THE FRIEND

On the place of Miss Jane Frost
There was a gully no one crossed,
    It was not the lambkill there,
    Not the dark pools everywhere.

Round-eyed boys had come across her
Putting out a parlor saucer
    Full of milk there, and next day
    The milk was all licked clean away.

In among the brackish runnels
There were many grassy tunnels,
    Not made by mice, but something thicker,
    Long and strong, quieter, quicker.

In a gully sun shines hot,
Hot gullies breed things folks best not
    Know too well by bush and stone
    If folks are old and live alone.

Miss Frost had her friend, they said,
Why, she had never gone to bed
    In her house where nothing stirred
    Until she got the proper word.

And she would go to sleep all day
Standing right upon her way
    If the friend she so well knew
    Happened to up and tell her to.

A woman who will go to sleep
On the road is one to keep
    On the other side of the road
    When you go light or under load.

Passersby would hear Jane talk
When she was boiling her Sunday cock,
    Hear her ask the way to do it,
    Though every last grown woman knew it.

Sometimes she sang an old hymn tune,
Slim as the April, thin new moon,
  But someone called the lines before
  She sent them out of her empty door.

It was not a pleasant thing
To hear an old, old woman sing
  Without any company,
  It made the heart beat hard's could be.

Folks heard Jane ask the way to sweep
Her room and heard the woman weep
  And say how sorry she was she made
  Mistakes in sweeping, if they stayed.

People did not stay much, though,
Most people went a good stone's throw
  From her cottage as they passed.
  Smoke left her chimney's top at last.

The men found Jane past all relief,
Shrunken almost past belief
  In her bed, cold as the cover,
  Cold as the yellowed sheets above her.

Nobody knew how old Jane was,
Nobody living knew the cause
  Why Jane died or even when,
  At her funeral were only men.

The minister made the shortest shift,
The casket was not much to lift,
  They carried it to the older yard
  And dug a place that dug blamed hard.

They put her in, they acted worried,
They shovelled the soil in, and they hurried,
  But when they were three-quarters through,
  They stopped and listened, the whole crew.

For between that shovel and this
The diggers heard a low long hiss,
    And out of the briars and the brake
    Slid a four-foot night-black snake.

The men threw down their tools and ran,
Every last big raw-boned man,
    And one swore he had looked around
    And seen the snake squirm into the ground.

They went and had a look next day,
There was a big hole in the clay,
    The men went home then fast as sin,
    They never filled the grave-hole in.

It was the last grave ever made
On that hill. Someone who strayed
    Up there once came on a blue
    Parlor saucer broken in two.

Sam Hall must be the happiest man
From Bath to Popham Dunes,
Everybody said, for Sam
Made up such sweet hymn tunes.

His head was full of them, a book
Was full of them as well,
A man who was so full of songs
Was happy, folks could tell.

And one day Sam Hall climbed his roof
With a rope and tied it
Round his chimney, and he noosed
His wrinkled neck inside it.

There would be an end to all
This misery called his brain,
His eaves would hang with happier
Burden than the rain.

Sam slid smiling towards the end
Of human ills and aches,
But suddenly his legs spread out,
And he put on the brakes.

One hymn tune more had come to him
Burning for release,
So Sam stopped upon the thin
Edge of night and peace.

He loosened up the noose and climbed
Down to ink and pen,
Immersed in music, he forgot
To climb back up again.

For years the noose hung on his eaves,
Each man who passed there swore,
"If I was happy as Sam Hall,
I'd never ask for more!"

THE SISTERS

Zenobia and Annie Lee
Were different as two worlds can be.

Zenobia was stiff as stubble,
But Sister Ann was limp as trouble.

Yet misfortune made them one
When their prayers were said and done.

They kept spinster hall together
In old age's Winter weather.

Before they plumped into Winter sheets,
They sat upon their haircloth seats.

They sat in nightgowns brushed and clean
With their oil-stove in between.

They warmed their shins and said their prayers,
With Summer in between their chairs.

When they were toasted through, they fled
And dived as one into the bed.

But one night, when the bucket froze,
Both sisters fell into a doze.

Zenobia forgot to keep
An eye on Ann, she fell asleep.

And Annie, as she always did,
Into a lovely cat-nap slid.

Jack Frost had painted every pane
When Zenoby came to life again.

She sat up guilty with a start,
She saw a sight that froze her heart.

Across the way, in her fine chair,
A huge fat Negress slumbered there!

Zenoby screamed in mortal fright,
Ann woke to a fearful sight.

Across from her a Negress sat
Yowling like a midnight cat!

The only bright things in her head
Were eyes and a vast mouth of red.

So facing this unearthly black,
Annie screamed her loudest back.

Zenobia yelled with all her soul
When she saw two eyeballs roll.

When she saw that red mouth gape,
She was in a Bedlam shape.

So they sat, and scream on scream
Roused the neighbors out of dream.

They came running and burst in
And found two sisters black as sin.

The sisters sat in sooty space
Screaming in each other's face.

The oil-stove had gone on a bust
And filled the air with carbon dust.

It had turned New England white
Into the Congo's darkest night.

It took the neighbors nearly till
Dawn to get the sisters still.

They soothed them, soaped them, scrubbed them fast,
Made them New England folks at last.

They put to bed these ancient two
Made one by fear and dusky hue.

RETURN JONATHAN

If he had searched a dozen books
And run off his two legs,
He couldn't have found a better name—
Return Jonathan Meigs.

It isn't every man who has
A history for a name,
When times had gotten dark for him,
His name had been a flame.

His father loved a pretty girl
Who had a tilted nose
Which somehow always made him think
Of a briar rose.

And Ann was like a briar rose
And thorny to the touch,
She was sharp with Jonathan,
She loved the youth so much.

But Jonathan was milkweed seed
And careless as white clover,
So one prickly day Ann up
And threw young Jonathan over.

Jonathan saddled up his mare,
Took his old guitar,
Said goodbye, and rode away
Into the evening star.

Ann tried her hardest to forget,
But she ached for the man.
She wrote, and her whole letter was:
"Return, Jonathan!"

And Jonathan returned and wed.
Few sons have a begetter
So lucky he could name his boy
A whole and handsome letter!

THE LAST PRISONER

The last man in Aurora's jail
Stayed a good long time,
He kept house there till most folks
Clean forgot his crime.

A tottering graybeard or two
Said he'd killed his wife,
But that was before most citizens
Came wailing into life.

They moved the jail to the county seat,
But jailbird St. John Lowe
Found a loophole in the law
And decided not to go.

He insisted on his right
To stay where he had stood
Trial, if no one else could
Act jailer, then he would.

So the town fathers gave St. John
The key, and every night
After his busy day, St. John
Locked himself up right.

St. John demanded meals, of course,
His three meals were sent in,
He called for shingles when it rained,
For pants when he wore thin.

He asked for red geraniums
To give his home a shine.
No matter where he went, he kept
The law:—To bed at nine.

For years where plowmen sweat he took
His philosophic walks,
And when he came to die, the town
Provided him the box.

The hens of Captain Toothaker
Were extraordinary hens,
Fed only when the tide was high,
They grew amphibians.

They went down to the flats and scratched
For mussels and skip-fleas,
They walked as their sea-master walked
With sprung sea-going knees.

And what was most unusual
In these hens of all
Was their accommodating them
To curse of alcohol.

For alcohol was clearly curse
On the captain's life,
It had lost him three good boats,
Two sons, and his one wife.

But his biddies stayed and learned
To steer clear of their lord
When the flame was in his eyes
And whiskey was aboard.

Yet even hens amphibian
And schooled in drink's dark woe
Had to go to quarters in
The month of spitting snow.

So Christmas Eve found them inside
The barn when drink possessed
Their master and he thought it time
His Yuletide meat were dressed.

The captain went out with his light,
His axe, his Christmas cheer,
He called his biddies, but not one
Biddy would come near.

So Captain Toothaker put by
His suave and kindly air,
He cornered his mistrustful flock,
Hen after scared hen there.

And hen on hen across the block
He threw and swung with might
His axe at each hen's neck and threw
Each biddy into the night.

But alcohol had blurred his eye,
As the alcohol will,
Each blow foreshortened, and he cut,
Not the neck, but bill.

Every hen that hit the floor
Rose with gory screams
And flew, she never knew just how,
Up to the barn's top beams.

God only knows what din arose
In that old barn-loft then,
Neighbors miles around were roused,
Came running, boys and men.

And such a sight as met their eyes!—
A captain, chastened, bland,
Chucking to his sky-high hens
With corns in his big hand.

Hens that never once again
Would peck up yellow seed
Aghast by lantern light and red
With the captain's deed!

"Bid-bid-biddies, here, bid-bid!"
To heaven rose his cries,
And on the rafters bill-less birds
With horror in their eyes.

The neighbors had to run and fetch
Their shotguns and let go,
They brought the marred hens down in rags
To end the squalls and woe.

At every shot, the stars came through
The old barn's rotted side,
They left the captain deep in rags
And shards of Christmas-tide.

THE PRESCRIPTION

Master Nehemiah Potts
Gave his crew good care,
Whatever ailed a sailorman,
He had the right cure there.

Bottle Nine upon his shelf
Was rich in vital irons,
Number Eight was remedy
For Barcelona sirens.

Five for gall-stones, Ten for spleen,
Six for cuts and smarts,
Four for broken heads, and Three
For the broken hearts.

This voyage, salt-horse was all they had,
Hardtack, and weevilled beans,
The men upon the yards all looked
Empty in their jeans.

Sam Given came to Master Potts,
Wobblecropped and shaky,
"What ails you, lad?" the master roared.
"My stomach, Sir. It's achy."

The master ran his knotty thumb
Through his dog-eared book.
"For stomach troubles, here I find
Seventeen must be took."

He took Seventeen from the shelf,
But Seventeen was dry.
The master took two others down,
A great light in his eye.

"By my reckoning, Nine and Eight
Make Seventeen. Drink, lad!"
And Sam ran out with a belly full
Of sirens ironclad!

Houses came down the yellow waves,
The khaki men sweat blood,
Chickens sailed on rolling coops,
Missouri roared at flood.

Barns uprooted, brindle cows
Swam with lifted head,
A mother rocked with her small child
On the family bed.

The soldiers waded in hip-boots
Across a drowning farm
And burst in through the cabin door
To save a man from harm.

He would not come, he clenched his hands
Around his chimney's girth,
He bit the hands they laid on him,
"I will not leave this hearth!"

The soldiers left the man at last,
They watched his roof go under.
"I bet he had a roll of bills
Below that hearth, by thunder!"

When the flood crept back and left
The cabin's ruined room,
They found the man sprawled in the mud
Face down and cold as doom.

They used their crowbars on the hearth
And broke apart the stones
To find the hoard he died to keep.
They found a hound-dog's bones.

CURIOSITY

Curiosity, they say,
Killed many a good cat in its day.

Three mountain boys spanked down their curls,
Scrubbed ears, and went to call on girls.

Spring was in the mountain pines,
But rain came down like pitchfork tines.

They sat inside, Dan, John, and Mose,
Jen, Moll, and May, in two prim rows.

When it grew late, pa took the light
And said the boys must stay the night.

He showed the suitors up the ladder,
The boys undressed, growing sadder, sadder.

They settled on the husks, they tried
To sleep, but their blue eyes were wide.

For down below a giggling spread,
Up went the ears on each boy's head.

The boys crept to the loft's edge there,
Cornhusks bristled in their hair.

The girls were busy at the hearth
Bubbling over in their mirth.

The young men leaned out farther still,
And then the floor-planks leaned downhill.

Mose and John and Dan upended
And all at once head-first descended.

Down they plunged and landed flush
In the kettle of hot mush.

Three young, red men without breeches
Danced the hearth with Choctaw screeches.

The girls fell backward in wild throes,
The three red suitors found their clothes.

Three young suitors, hot with pain,
Vamoosed in the healing rain.

Love flew off that mountain top
Two counties before it made a stop.

Twelve Androscoggin bridges gone,
The river came like the Amazon
Downhill and piled the blue ice in,
The last bridge twanged like a fiddle-string.

The railroad bridge leaned slow and gave
And plunged into its dark green grave,
The ice-cakes roared through the tall trees
And brought the forest to its knees.

The pulpwood went like twelve-inch shells
Through the pulpmill's walls, and hells
Of water filled the Frenchtown shacks,
Whole families rode their houses' backs.

So Anne LeBel came to her hour,
With wild wavetops in white flower
Outside her upstairs window there,
And bore her husband his fine heir.

The father and the priest rowed to
The window, took the mother through
With the new son at her breast,
And rowed off to a drier nest.

When they christened Anne's stout son,
They chose for name the fittingest one
For one whose bed was bare of roses,
"We christen thee by name of Moses!"

Two up-country whiskered men
Had swopped things all their life,
One was a widower, and one had
Married a brand-new wife.

Widower Talbot thought and thought
About friend Trufant's Nance,
And he felt younger thirty years
And fit to lead a dance.

He had a pretty mare named Kate,
Quicksilver to the spur,
Tom Trufant for the last four months
Had cast sheep's eyes at her.

"What say we make a swop of it,
Your Nance for my mare Kate?"
Tom Trufant's adam's apple stuck,
Temptation was so great.

He found his voice at last, but it
Was low down at its root.
"My Nance is far too fine a wife,
Throw something in to boot."

Will Talbot thought of Nancy's plump
Young arms and pretty chin,
He thought about her cheeks, and threw
His Mexican saddle in.

"You'll have to throw in more," said Tom.
"All right," said Will, "by God,
This will have to do you, Tom,
I'll have the young mare shod!"

So shod Kate was and saddled, too,
Tom rode off with a tune,
And Will went in to comb his beard
For his second honeymoon.

THE SEVEN VIRGINS OF KAMCHATKA

Catharine, Empress of Muscovy,
For all her wit, did never know
How very wide her realm was till
Seven virgins showed her it was so.

When her highway to the east
Reached Kamchatka and the sea,
"Guardsmen, go!" she cried, "and fetch
Seven Kamchatka maids to me.

"Seven virgins, pure as down
Of ptarmigan and innocent,
Bring from my Pacific shore."
And seven handsome Guardsmen went.

The Empress waited. Seven maids
And seven Guardsmen travelled west,
The birches spread and shed their leaves,
Then rumor broke the Empress' rest.

Word came how the slim white girls
Were nothing like as slim's they'd been,
The Empress' head was a thunderhead,
She sent for seven other men.

"Captains of my Bodyguard!
Sharpen swords, shine up your gears,
Ride and bring seven Guardsmen's heads
Sliced off even with the ears!"

Now Guards rode east, and Guards rode west,
Birch trees blossomed by the road,
Seven fine Guardsmen, two feet long,
In the sunlight kicked and crowed.

"The days grow long, my Bodyguard
Are gone a long time on the way,
My people grow impatient now
For our Pacific holiday."

Seven Guardsmen's handsome heads
Dangled neatly in the air,
Seven virgins still rode west,
But fourteen Guardsmen now rode there.

Fast as handsome horses go
Jingled the growing cavalcade,
Nowhere did they stop to rest
By mountain, vale, or birches' shade.

And word came when the first snow flew,
And Catharine's eyes like fires shone:
The new-moon slenderness once more
In her seven maids was gone.

The trumpets blew, the red wine flowed,
Kamchatka came to Peter's town,
The Empress stood up lily-tall,
A smile broke through her regal frown.

"Seven Guardsmen I sent forth,
But if my good eyes do not lie,
Twenty-one Guardsmen, long or short,
In the street are riding by.

"Ah well, the fault is Muscovy's,
She is so wide, a squad of men
Who ride with virgins may well be
A regiment when they come again!"

SAL'S SINKERS

Captain Jonathan Stover sat
Toasting his gray woolen feet
Before the galley-stove, there was
Fog, and nothing to do but eat.

He was having a mug-up on
Sal's sinkers and deep-apple pie,
All dories save the one astern
Were on the *Sal's* deck high and dry.

The Grand Banks fog was thick pea-soup,
John had a doughnut at his mouth,
But did not swallow it, his wide
Tanned Maine ear leaned suddenly south.

John never took another bite,
He did not pull his hip-boots on,
He said no word to any man,
He dropped his doughnut, he was gone.

The crew rushed up in time to see
Captain Jonathan jump in the dory
Riding astern, and cut the line,
They heard his oarlocks creak like glory.

The codfish men stood open-mouthed,
The oars of their master dimmed away.
Then there was another sound,
And a sabre took shape in the gray.

A sabre sharp as a fish-hawk's wing
Came on them from the top of the sky,
It cut the schooner clean in two,
They heard a continent hissing by.

They pitched up mountains in the fog,
Mountains subsided, silence fell,
They swam in icy gloom, and then
They heard the sound they knew so well.

Oarlocks creaking, coming fast,
Then Captain Stover, "Here you be!
I knowed I had to look alive,
But no Cunarder can fool me!

"Lucky thing I was below
And heard that baby through the waves,
Or we'd be fifty fathoms down
Picking out some pretty graves."

One by one, they climbed aboard,
Manned the oars and made them hiss.
"Head for Halifax!" John cried,
"Thank God and Sally's sinkers for this!"

THE HARVEST

Whatever corn or oats they reaped,
One crop New England farmers heaped.

They could bet their marrow-bones
Their fields would bear good crops of stones.

No matter how they gleaned them out,
Up another lot would sprout.

Size of a man's head, size of a cup,
Every Winter brought them up.

Thousands of them, bright and new,
Once the heaving frost was through.

Strange, earth's skeleton could be
Made of so many vertebrae!

Yet Nature, as usual, up and found
A way to beat stones underground.

The old dame takes a mid-position,
Her meat and drink is competition.

So laws of compromise began
A secret way of helping man.

The farmers grew so stout a lot
Boys on boys their bodies got.

He was but middling of such men
Who mustered only nine or ten.

The boys went out and cleared the fields
Of their annual frosty yields.

They piled ten thousand miles of rocks
In walls around their cabbage stalks.

They walled the weeds and wild outside
All their tipped-up countryside.

When they had finished, in elation
They went west and built a nation,

Built up cities in the plain,
Built cathedrals for the grain,

Broke the Rocky Mountains' bones,
These sons of hard New England stones!

THE TREEING OF THE ELDER

Jim was nine and full of glee,
The laughingest boy in Tennessee,
He could not keep his laughing in
Even in church where it was sin.

Jim's pappy vowed that he would tan
Jim's backsides if his laughter ran
Over in church one evening more,
That was his final word, he swore.

Wednesday night, the organ's wheeze
And fifty Methodists on their knees,
And in came Jim with big-toes wide,
Leaving his coon-dog Spot outside.

He did not want his trousers heated,
He passed the boys where they were seated,
Jim wanted to be safe, and so
He went down to the old men's row.

He wedged himself between two tall
Men with beards like a waterfall,
Wedged his small thighs in with sober
Pants as grave as old October.

Elder Harte, big as the world,
Went out to lead the prayers, unfurled
His snowy whiskers like a ram's
And got down on his massive hams.

He cried out on old Satan's guile,
And who should come trotting up the aisle
But Spot, the hunter of mountain coons,
His eyes were big as hunter-moons.

He went up to the praying one,
He smelt him, then his white teeth shone,
The hairs stood on him stiff and stark,
Spot crouched, then Spot began to bark.

He yapped behind the Elder's seat,
Amazed at plenteousness of meat,
He was at loss, think as he might,
Where to take his foremost bite.

Jim whistled low, Spot did not heed him,
He circled Elder Harte, he treed him,
Bark on bark. Then Jim let out
Snort on snort and shout on shout.

He knew his pants would catch rawhide
But could not stop, and then each side
Noah and Abram let out two
Snorts that shook Jim through and through.

The patriarchs threw back their old
Heads and roared till the tears rolled,
Jim knew his seat would wear no marks—
Pap could not spank the patriarchs!

WHITE HORSES OF SHARON

No mutton, veal, or beef to roast
In the Castle of the Holy Ghost.

Potatoes, corn were running low,
And belts went in a notch or so.

A hundred babies and one cow!
There was no horse to pull the plow.

The faithful spaded dawn to dark,
But their eyes had lost the spark.

In the North Tower, on his knees,
A man was praying without cease.

In the South, the women prayed,
Relieved like sentries, wife or maid.

But knees were sore, and no light came
Over the pinewoods flame on flame.

Elijah, who was born Seth Jones,
Spent days upon his raw knee-bones.

He wore his pants through to his skin,
He swore his flock were steeped in sin.

God had sent the help before
When wolves of Winter nosed the door.

Hadn't a hundred barrels of flour
Come when he had set the hour?

Hadn't the widow's son been healed
When he touched him in the field?

When had God not kept the word
He spoke and His Elijah heard?

They were men of doubt and sin!
The Prophet smote his Yankee chin.

But his people murmured still.
They'd brought good money up the hill.

When they left a world turned bad,
They gave Elijah all they had.

This man his acres, this his cow,
This one his hens. Where were they now?

Elijah promised milk and honey
For their nest-eggs of hard money.

He said Jehovah would provide!
Dan Snow was out at his backside.

Jane Witherspoon was on her uppers,
Where were the corn and wine and suppers?

"O ye sinners hell may burn!
God scorns not naked feet or stern.

"Ye sigh for Egypt's fleshpots still.
But God forgives. Now hear His will!

"Ye cry to Him for help to plow,
And God has sent His horses now!

"Go, two of you, to Bethel Town,
And take the largest harnesses down.

"Go to the Freight House, ye will see
The white span God has sent to me!"

The men went with a trembling tread,
And it was as Elijah said.

At the Freight House was a span
Of horses to amaze a man.

White as tall twin thunder showers,
Huge of hock, soft-eyed as flowers.

When they brought them home, the walls
Of Sharon shook as with trumpet calls.

The faithful lined the place ten deep,
The men to cheer, the wives to weep.

They burst into a hymn full-throat.
Elijah put away the note:

Received, S. Jones, two-hundred cash
For two matched Percherons.   John Nash.

He locked the drawer, he came out bland,
He blessed his flock with lifted hand.

They hitched the horses up, the sod
Came open like the palm of God.

The furrows ran up to the sky,
The span glowed hot as they reared high.

There was no stopping them to rest,
They sliced the world from east to west.

Unwearied, they rolled on like thunder,
They turned the hungry sand hills under.

Their great hooves dashed dry stones away,
Where their hooves smote was blue clay.

The fire flew beneath their feet,
They woke the cold earth with their heat.

The faithful sprinkled on the seeds,
Up shot the corn, too thick for weeds.

The corn spread over them like tents,
Its silk plumes smelled of frankincense.

The crop was the largest ever seen,
The land groaned under gold and green.

When the harvest moon rolled in,
Corn and wheat bulged every bin.

Still the horses came, and still
Corn rolled till it crossed the sill.

Still the horses arched their necks
And brought the grain in pecks on pecks.

Men built new barns, the ears still flowed
Into the new barns load on load.

There was a ham on every beam,
The babies swam in milk and cream.

Jane Witherspoon had shoes with soles,
Dan Snow had trousers without holes.

The grapes hung low down as they durst,
The crickets sang until they burst.

When the frost fell on the Fall,
The horses brought last loads of all.

It was pumpkins, giant ones,
The cart was loaded down with suns.

The sky-sun tipped the western trees,
And there came strange belated bees.

They stung the horses, and the span
Frothed with fire, broke, and ran.

They ran straight at the sun, and gold
Pumpkins bounced and pumpkins rolled.

The earth was pumpkins rolling bright
Across the stubble towards the night.

88

The world was pumpkins rolling fast,
The horses hit the sun at last.

The last men saw of them, they broke
Into the sun-disk and were smoke.

Up in the holy highest tower
Elijah sat white as a flower.

His face was blanched with fear and awe,
He read the letter in his paw:

We have the horses and have your cash,
Where shall we deliver?—J. Nash.

The room was full of the strange bees,
Elijah slid upon his knees.

"God forgive me, wretched sinner!"
And he went down to the harvest dinner.

AROOSTOOK

Land of the potato-blossom's lace
And honey-bees brimming all space,
Where boys are running everywhere,
And all like sunlight on their hair.

Country where the children seem
All boys, and blond ones, and each stream
Shines with them and comes alive
As naked boys leap up and dive.

Land where green potatoes. meet
The sky at east and west, and sweet
Red clover blossoms, and the bees
Take the place of murmuring seas.

Wide horses come down every hill,
Behind their flanks the blue clouds spill
Out in parallel small showers
Over the potato-flowers.

Land of barns half under earth,
Barns all bursting in their girth
With big barrels full of life,
Land where wind is like a knife.

Country of the highest thunder
And houses turning white in under,
Golden hilltops ten-miles long
Against blue mountains older than song.

Land of snowdrifts six-foot high
And dead men dancing on the sky
Hand in hand on August nights,
Diamond land of northern lights.

Land of men built big and sunny,
Land of spruces, mustard, honey,
Aroostook! pith and starch of Maine,
Hotter than all gilded Spain!

"Minerva, you have been the wife
Of Thomas White here twenty years,
And now you come before this Court
To divorce him, it appears."

"Yes, Suh, Judge, I does for suttin.
I'se at the limit of muh rope."
"Well, Minerva, you have reasons
For such a serious step, I hope."

"I has, Judge."—"Has Tom ever failed
To support you and provide?"
"No, Suh. They always was bacon
To grease muh fry-pan when I fried."

"Did your husband ever beat you?
Hit or slap or hurt you bad?"
"I reckon not. He'd not be this hyeah
Healthy nigger if he had."

"Then why do you come to this Court
And ask divorce if this is so?"
"I tells you, Judge, it's just like this—
I cyan't stand this man's taste no mo'!"

HEN DODDER

Hen Dodder was a civic pride
Like Wilton's big town-clock,
The clock was slower than the time,
Hen matched it in his walk.

Hen was tall and bunion-boned,
His gnarled shoulders stooped,
His gates-ajar moustache turned down,
Everything on Hen drooped.

He did not do much regular work,
He hayed a bit for people,
Laid up a stonewall here or there,
Or painted the church steeple.

He did jobs others did not want,
He lived from hand to mouth,
His trousers left a lot of Hen's
Ankles to the south.

Folks always smiled when Hen was named
In the grocery talks,
They had a nickname for the man,
They called him "God's off-ox."

He always came a little late,
He always sat quite dumb
Till the subject had been changed,
And then he'd argue some.

But Wilton menfolks, just the same,
Were proud of Hen's low stammer,
He could talk just like a book,
And he was up on grammar.

Hen knew grammar to the roots,
He could floor the teachers,
His words came out like *Bible* ones,
Bigger than the preacher's.

And Hen could take the travelling men's
Money at draw-poker,
He always dressed his best for cards
In Sunday pants and choker.

But checkers were his greatest gift:
Hen would sit and stare
An hour long without a stir
At the checkers there.

Then all at once his knotty, long
Middle finger flew
Out across the board and moved,
And his foe was through.

Champions from other towns
Came, and came to grief,
Their adam's apples rose and fell
In stark unbelief.

Hen lived alone and cooked his meals,
He talked to none but men,
Wilton people vowed there was
Only one of Hen.

And in his forty-seventh year
Hen married Soony Blake,
He'd never noticed a girl before
This one lean as a rake.

The men all joked Hen on his luck,
His wedding and his bedding,
They said they always knew a good
Rooster by his treading.

Hen said nothing, but he now
Took to working steady,
When Soony got home from the mill,
She found the supper ready.

Hen washed and swept and kept the house
Clean as a willow whistle,
His step quickened up, and Hen
Seemed new and full of gristle.

He never touched a checkerboard,
He gave the store wide berth,
Wilton men saw in Hen's eyes
A light not seen on earth.

And that September, Soony stayed
A week home from her loom
And bore a son to Hen, who looked
Like an apple bloom.

Folks said that after this event
Hen grew a little loony,
The sun for Hen came up and set
In the boy and Soony.

Hen's moustache turned a little up
At its gangling points,
His trousers rounded out a bit
On his bony joints.

Soony grew thinner year by year
In the dusty mill,
But she stayed home to rest at last
Because Hen's child was ill.

It was rickets, Doctor said,
The thin boy died next day,
Soony went back to her loom
And worked her strength away.

Hen stayed home and did not cook
Or sweep much more at all.
Soony finished work for good,
And died last day of Fall.

Then all at once old Hen came back
As though he'd never gone,
The same old rambling, shuffling Hen
The sun had shone upon.

He talked grammar, and his long
Fingers moved the men,
Hen stripped the drummers, and his words
Were *Bible* words again.

Some folks said that Hen was glad
His wife was in her box,
Hen was Hen, and what could you
Expect of "God's off-ox?"

And some folks found Hen in his barn
Sitting calm and splendid,
His head was fast inside a noose,
And his neck extended.

Hen had fixed things on his feet
And spread his legs apart,
He sat down quietly to rest
His big and broken heart.

MAINE GOES UP OR DOWN

Maine goes up or down a hill,
The pastures run down deep and still,
The sea is uphill like a wall
Cool and azure over all.

It does not matter where men stand,
There is bright water, there is bright land
Under toes of shoes they wear
And wild wings scissoring the air.

A man is always high, high up,
He walks the sharp rim of a cup
Full of sparkling waves or people,
His next step may be over a steeple.

His next step may be over a bay,
He walks with boats along his way,
He goes lightly lest he crush
White farmhouses or the evening thrush.

Maine is all things steep and far,
Maybe a lighthouse, maybe a star
Is underfoot each boy who brings
The cows home with his feet all wings.

GHOST HOUSE

When Holly Howard bought the house,
Old as weather, picked as bone,
He thought it vacant, but he found
That he was not to be alone.

One night he found he'd left his plane
While he was putting things to rights,
He thought of the lockless kitchen door,
And how he'd missed some tools there nights.

The front door had a brand-new lock,
And Holly did not have his key,
So he went in the rearward way
Stepping as quiet as could be.

But with the first step Holly took,
A step upstairs joined his below,
His footfalls crossed the darkling rooms,
Above, he heard the others go.

Ah, now I've got the scalawag
Who stole my hatchet!—Holly glowed,
He walked as light as though on eggs,
Upstairs the feet went light and slowed.

Holly seized a piece of beam
And stood upon the second stair,
The locked front doorway at his back,
He felt cold water drench his hair.

The steps came downward in the dark,
Holly raised his club on high,
The footfalls reached the second tread,
He felt it sag. . . . A sigh went by.

One leap, and the astounded man
Swept wide the locked door with his right,
Bits of Yale and Towne flew far,
And he was out in the safe night.

He ran to old Bill Hummer's place,
His eyes upon the end of his nose.
"There's someone funny in my house,
He came downstairs right on my toes!"

"How," said Bill, "did the thing get past?—
There's no room on those stairs for two."
Holly Howard swallowed hard,
"He didn't go round me. He went through!"

"Oh, that's all right," said Bill, "don't fret,
That one inside's a friendly ghost,
He wouldn't hurt a fly. It's ones
Outside that you will dread the most."

"Good God!" cried Howard, "is my house
Crammed with spooks up to the eaves?"
"Well," Bill answered, "there's the lady
In the buttery who grieves.

"Then there's the lady in the attic
Who plays the organ that ain't there.
We used to listen, when we was kids,
Each Sunday eve, and she played rare.

"But it's the hants that work outdoors
You have to watch. John says they're mean.
When you bought John out, did you
Take a good look at John McKeen?"

"Why, yes, he's got the shakes, his head
Keeps bobbing up and down a dight."
"You look again," said Bill, "you'll find
He nods his head from left to right."

"Why so?" asked Holly. "Well, you see,
John had three windows he must check
In all his rooms, all through his nights,
And it disorganized his neck.

"There's one room has four windows, which
Was just too much for poor old John.
The fourth one in his sitting-room
He up and nailed the shutters on.

"And have you seen John's shotgun yet?
Both barrels on it are paper-thin—
He shot the thing so many nights,"
Said Hummer with an ear-wide grin.

"Whatever for?"—Said Bill, "He had
To keep those ghosts outside at bay.
At midnight he shot down the front,
And then he shot the other way."

"What was he after?"—"Plenty!" cried
Old Bill. "Unless the poor man shot,
There would have been ten Indians
Grinning in on him red-hot."

"Indians?—For God's sake, man,
How come such things as Indians there?"
"It's a long story," said his friend,
"A sad one, too, of blood and hair.

"The builder of your house, James Cain,
Had a wife he doted on,
One day, three hundred years ago,
He came home, and he found her gone.

"But she had not gone far. James saw
His woman through the window panes,
She was burning like white hell,
Stuck full of pine and powder-grains.

"And Abenakis dyed blood-red,
And some all painted yellow and blue,
Were dancing round the fiery wife
Hoping her man would come out, too.

"But James Cain took his musket down,
Loaded it up with shingling-nails,
He let go through the window panes,
The Red Men left with wildcat wails.

"When James ran out to his dead wife,
He found her hair gone every bit.
James took an oath that he would have
Ten horsehair scalps to pay for it.

"James got three scalps that year, and then
Quebec fell, the peace was signed,
But James was loaded up for bear,
He got his scalps, he did not mind.

" 'See here, my man, the war is done.
We buy no scalps. You cannot sell.'
'Keep your bounty, Mr. Clerk,
I'll scalp, and you can go to hell.'

"So the years went, and no braves
Could feel safe on their beds at night
Till they had sent out scouts to see
James go to bed and douse his light.

"Poor critters! no one told them when
James squared the count up and was gone.
So even after they died, too,
They still stayed scared and kept right on.

"They scared old John half out of what
Little wits the poor man had—
Red, painted faces peering in,
They sure kinked up John's neckbone bad!

"They must have thought that John was James.
I think they're harmless," Hummer said.
"But John he thanks his God each night
He has his hair still on his head!"

100